Lift Your Light a Little Higher

The Story of Stephen Bishop: Slave-Explorer

Heather Henson

ILLUSTRATED BY
Bryan Collier

atheneum

A Caitlyn Dlouhy Book
ATHENEUM BOOKS FOR YOUNG READERS
New York · London · Toronto · Sydney · New Delhi

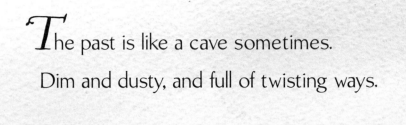

The past is like a cave sometimes.
Dim and dusty, and full of twisting ways.

Not an easy thing to journey down. 'Specially
when you're searching out a path that's hardly
been lit, a trail that's never been smooth
or flat or plain to follow.

Don't worry, though. I know a few things
'bout leading folks around inside the dark,
showing off sights that have never been seen.
Stick close to me, and you won't get lost.

Think you're ready? All right then, here we go.

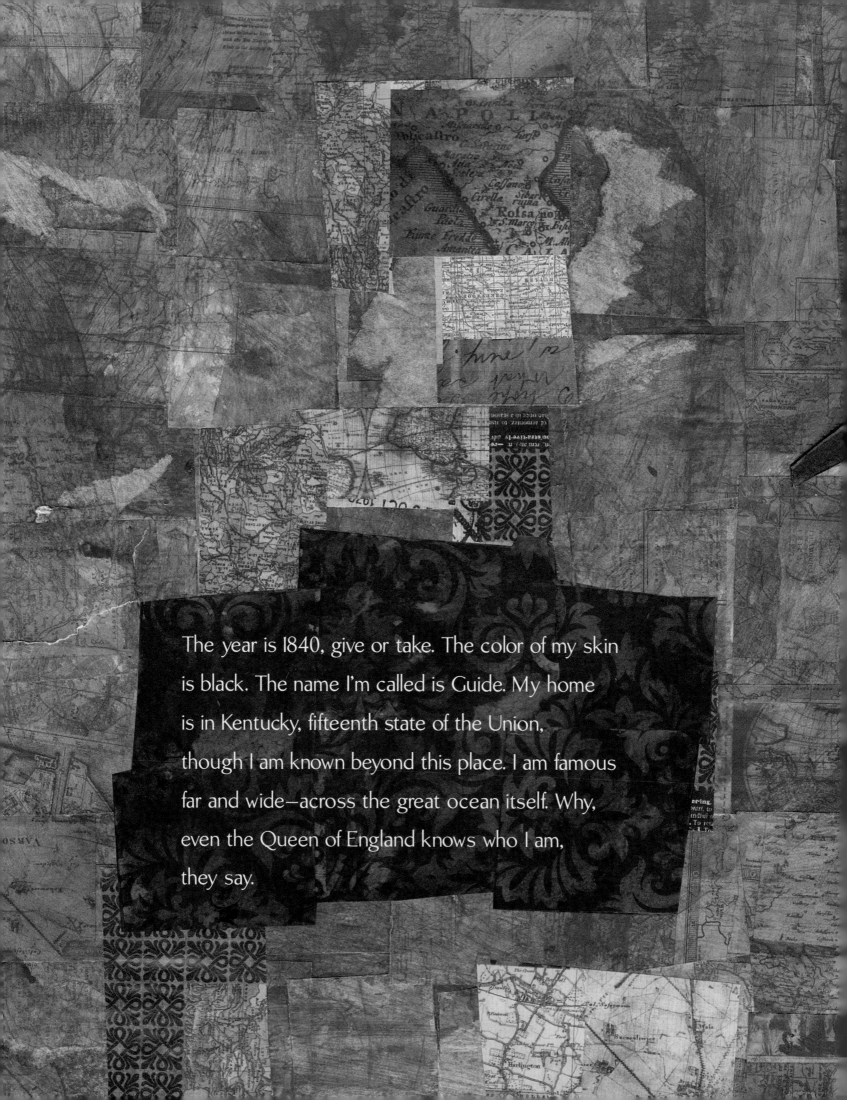

The year is 1840, give or take. The color of my skin
is black. The name I'm called is Guide. My home
is in Kentucky, fifteenth state of the Union,
though I am known beyond this place. I am famous
far and wide—across the great ocean itself. Why,
even the Queen of England knows who I am,
they say.

But being known is not the same as being free,
no sir. Famous or not, you will not find my story
written down exactly as it happened. Because
in 1840, in most states of this young nation,
it is against the law to teach me to read and write.

What's that? You take a stumble already?

You got a question so soon?

Why?

Is that what you want to know?

Why is it against the law to teach me

my letters?

Because I am a slave. Because I am the property of a white man. Because I am bought and sold, same as an ox or a mule; bought and sold, along with the land I work.

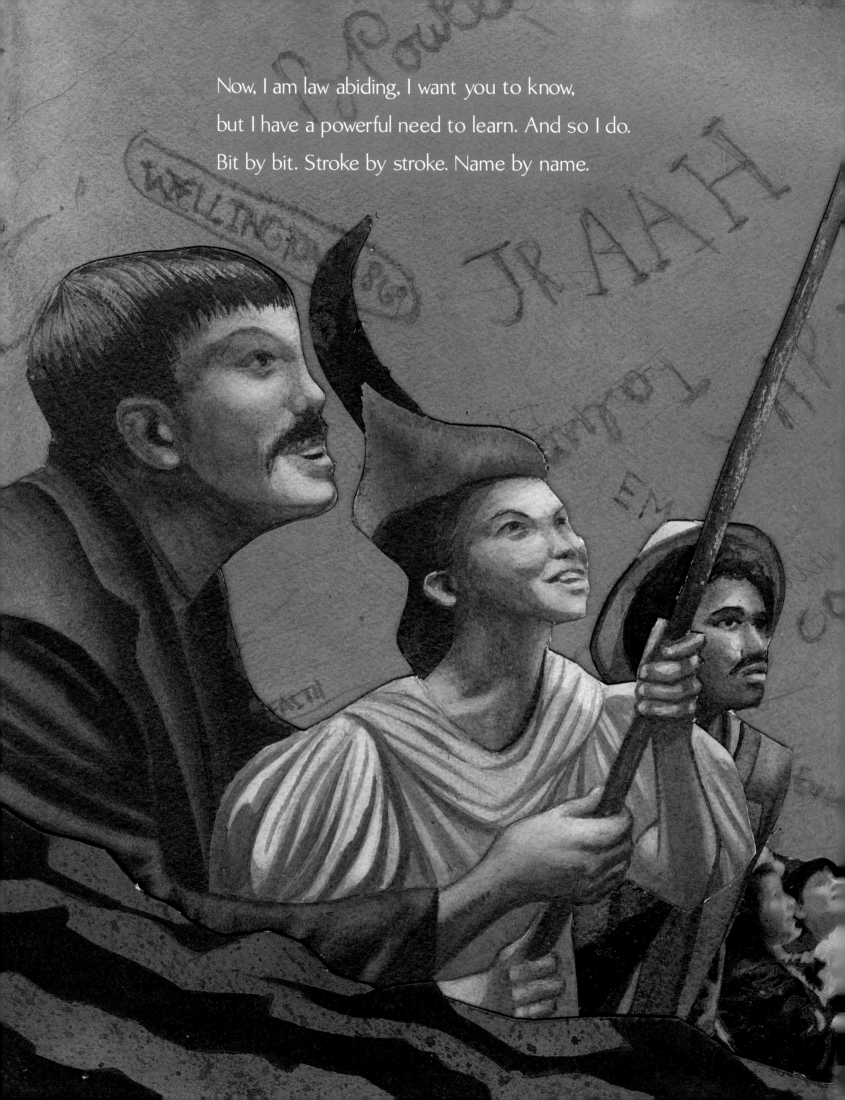

Now, I am law abiding, I want you to know,
but I have a powerful need to learn. And so I do.
Bit by bit. Stroke by stroke. Name by name.

All the fine folks passing through this place
want to leave their mark, and so I show them
how to candle-write a line as sure as ink.
And in return they teach me, sometimes,
without knowing what's been taught.

I learn by sight, and one day when I am ready,

I hold the candle up to write my own name,

there beside the rest. So that when you come

to this very spot—two hundred years from now—

you will see my mark right where

I left it:

S t e p h e n.

And you will have no way of knowing,

I'll tell you true, from candle smoke on

stone, the color of my skin, black or white.

They say a pioneer man discovered this place
out tracking bear. Of course, he was not the first.
There were others here. I've seen the proof myself.
I've held a deerskin moccasin in my palm,
a thing so old and small it makes me ponder
those times that came before. It makes me try
to figure what will be left of me, besides my name.
A lamp, a stick, a pair of boots so rough and worn,
you'll wonder at the path I walked to make them so.

I did not choose this path, of course, being a slave.
But sometimes I like to think this path chose me.

My master brought me here as a boy, and told me
to learn the ways of the cave well enough to lead
paying folks around inside the deep.

I learned the cave all right.
I know the twists
and turns; the secrets, too.

I am the first to lay eyes upon those eyeless fish,
those crawdads white as bone—wonders of nature!—
bound inside their hidden stream. I am the first
to cross what even learned men have deemed
uncrossable.

And I never do fear the dark, no sir. In fact,
I come to love it best down here, alone and still.
The fall of my own step, no other; the sound
of my own voice, should I choose to speak.
The glow of my own lamp 'luminating what's
never been lit, not since the dawn of time,
at least, the beginning of every thing.

Down here, I am Guide—a man able to walk
before other men, not behind; a man able to school
even the brightest scholar; a man able to bring
a crowd of folks deep into the belly of the earth
and back again, safe and sound. A man—
down here, that's what I am—a man,
not just a slave.

In time, I have a wife whose name I leave
for all to see. In time, we have a son.
In time, my master says we shall be free,
us three. But time is not always a friend,
no sir. That's what I've found. Time
does not wait for us; time does not wait
for much. Why, even deep inside the cave,
water will turn to stone, in time.

No history book can tell exactly how
I died, or why. But I will say this:
I never left the cave. I am here still.

My name. My spirit. My story.

Maybe not the life you were expecting.
Maybe not a tale you've always known.

But I warned you when we started out:
The journey back is dark and winding.
And sometimes you just got to lift your light
a little higher; sometimes you just got to go
beyond what's written down to get to what's
been left untold.

STEPHEN BISHOP was a slave. He was born in Kentucky around 1821, and as a teenager was brought by his master to work as a guide in Mammoth Cave.

Located in southwestern Kentucky, Mammoth Cave is the longest cave system in the world, with more than four hundred miles of mapped underground passageways. As early as 1825, Mammoth Cave was a busy tourist attraction. During Stephen's time, people traveled hundreds, even thousands, of miles—from big cities back East, from all over Europe, by railroad and steamship, and finally by stagecoach to the backwoods of Kentucky—simply to see the wonders of this great underground world.

There were several slave guides, but Stephen became the best known from around 1838 to 1857. Writers of the day who visited the cave mentioned Stephen's eloquence and intelligence, his deep knowledge of the cave, his important discoveries.

Stephen was the first to draw an extensive map of the cave and the first to cross a previously impassable chasm called the "Bottomless Pit." He was the first to discover a new species of eyeless fish and albino crawdads found only in the underground rivers of Mammoth Cave.

Despite all this, Stephen remained a slave almost until the very end of his life, bought and sold with the cave itself. Strangely, his death, at the relatively young age of thirty-seven, was barely noted, and how he died remains a mystery. His gravestone sits near the original entrance to Mammoth Cave.

After being privately owned and changing hands for nearly two hundred years, Mammoth Cave became a national park in 1946, and an International Biosphere Reserve in 1990. You can still visit the cave, as two million people do each year! (Go to nps.gov/maca/index.htm and mammothcave.com for information.) You can still follow the exact same tour Stephen gave, and you can still see his name and his wife's name—Charlotte—written in Stephen's very own hand alongside all the other "historical graffiti," created by holding a candle tied to a long taper to the ceiling of the cave.

In reality, not much is known about Stephen as a person. And so in this book, I tried to imagine his life inside the cave from a few written descriptions, from a few facts. In this book, I tried to imagine what Stephen Bishop, Cave Explorer and Guide, would have to say to us if history—if slavery—had not silenced him.

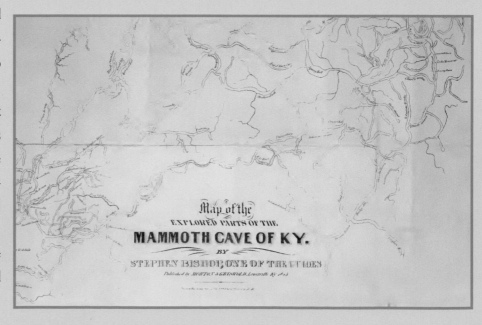

Map of the
EXPLORED PARTS OF THE
MAMMOTH CAVE OF KY.
BY
STEPHEN BISHOP, ONE OF THE GUIDES

ILLUSTRATOR'S NOTE

IN THE 1800S, THE MAMMOTH CAVES, located in eastern Kentucky, were a part of a plantation where mining for nitre took place and saltpetre was produced. Saltpetre, combined with sulphur and charcoal, was used to make high-grade gunpowder, which was dear as gold to those serving in the War of 1812. Once the war ended, however, so went the need for gunpowder. This transition gave birth to converting the caves to a prosperous touring business.

In the 1830s, a slave named Stephen Bishop was assigned the daunting task of seeking and discovering new passages in the depths of a dark and very dangerous cave system.

My goal for this book was to illuminate, with watercolor and collage, Stephen Bishop's savvy determination and courage, and the dignity and wit with which he steered countless tourists safely through the caves' dark passages, perhaps even discovering a glimpse of freedom there in the depths, where he was a leader.

As tourists hung on to every word Stephen spoke and direction that he gave, some wanted to leave their mark for future visitors by writing their names and dates on the walls and ceilings in candle smoke. Stephen Bishop taught himself to read and write by observing such acts. Looking upon his signature myself, I saw the mark of a man among others, not merely a slave.

RESOURCES

Bullitt, Alexander Clark. *Rambles in the Mammoth Cave, During the Year 1844, by a Visitor*. Louisville, KY: Morton and Griswold, 1845.

Burroughs, John. "In Mammoth Cave," Vol. 9 of *The Writings of John Burroughs, the Riverby Edition*. New York and Boston: Houghton Mifflin, 1894.

Lyons, Joy Medley. *Making Their Mark: The Signature of Slavery at Mammoth Cave*. Fort Washington, PA: Eastern National, 2006.

McCombs, Davis. *Ultima Thule*. Yale Series of Younger Poets. New Haven, CT: Yale University Press, 2000.

Mitchell, Elizabeth. *Journey to the Bottomless Pit: The Story of Stephen Bishop & Mammoth Cave*. New York: Scholastic, 2006.

*This book is dedicated to my family, of course (Tim, Lila, Theo, Daniel),
but also to all those voices silenced for so long, all those stories lost.*
—H. H.

*I dedicate this project to all men, women, boys, and girls who carry the spirit of exploration
and discovery, because your efforts and bravery help bring light to the world.*
—B. C.

ACKNOWLEDGMENTS

I would like to thank Elizabeth Orndorff. Her play, *Death by Darkness*, inspired me to learn more
about Stephen Bishop, and ultimately to write this book. I would also like to thank the authors of
the books I used in my research and gratefully acknowledge herein.
—H. H.

A special thanks to Vickie Carson, who served as my guide through Mammoth Cave, and
to the drama students of Marlboro High School in Marlboro, New York, for being wonderful
performers, breathing life into this re-creation as reference models for my art.
—B. C.

ATHENEUM BOOKS FOR YOUNG READERS
An imprint of Simon & Schuster Children's Publishing Division
1230 Avenue of the Americas, New York, New York 10020
Text copyright © 2016 by Heather Henson
Illustrations copyright © 2016 by Bryan Collier
Image of Stephen Bishop in author note courtesy of the Library of Congress:
[Stephen Bishop, Afro American guide of Mammoth Cave, Kentucky, half length portrait, facing front]. [Published, 1882] Image.
Retrieved from the Library of Congress, loc.gov/iten/93507462. (Accessed March 28, 2016.)
For information about special discounts for bulk purchases, please contact Simon & Schuster Special Sales
at 1-866-506-1949 or business@simonandschuster.com.
The Simon & Schuster Speakers Bureau can bring authors to your live event. For more information or to book an event,
contact the Simon & Schuster Speakers Bureau at 1-866-248-3049 or visit our website at www.simonspeakers.com.
Book design by Laurent Linn
The text for this book was set in Brinar Pro.
The illustrations for this book were rendered in watercolor and collage.
Manufactured in China
0616 SCP
First Edition
2 4 6 8 10 9 7 5 3 1
CIP data for this book is available from the Library of Congress.
ISBN 978-1-4814-2095-2
ISBN 978-1-4814-2096-9 (eBook)